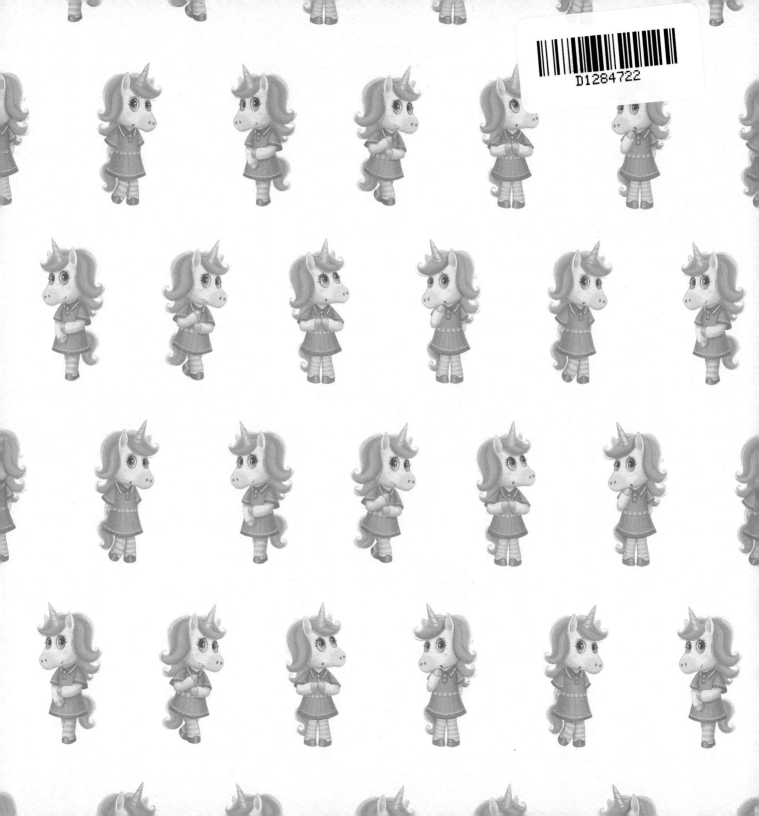

For Matthew
—R.L.U.

For Maira & Dastan
—Yusup

Petunia the Unicorn's Dazzling Christmas Debut
Copyright © 2021 by Waystation Media LLC

Published by But That's Another Story… Press
Ridgefield, CT

Printed in the United States of America.

First Printing, 2021.
ISBN: 978-1-953713-12-4
Library of Congress Control Number: 2021917611

Petunia the Unicorn's
Dazzling Christmas Debut

A Petunia Cupcake Fluffybottom Book

Written by R.L. Ullman
Illustrations by Yusup Mediyan

But That's
Another Story...
Press

My name is Petunia. My full name is Petunia Cupcake Fluffybottom. But I just go by Petunia.

This is my family. I live with my dynamic Auntie Sprinkles, my feisty dog Gumdrop, and our faithful butler Winston.

Life with Auntie Sprinkles is never dull. Her full name is Lady Rainbow Sprinkles Fluffybottom, but I just call her Auntie Sprinkles. She's very warm, very witty, and very, very wonderful.

She also has quite the appetite.

Gumdrop looks out for me. His bark is way bigger than his bite, but don't tell him I said that.

Even though Winston doesn't say much, he's always there when we need him. And I mean always.

This year we moved to Manhattan. We live in a brownstone on West 81st Street. I'm excited for our first Christmas in the city. Auntie Sprinkles loves to go over the top for the holidays, but since we're still new to the neighborhood, I was hoping she'd tone down the decorations this year.

She had other ideas.

She also decided to change out the furniture… again.

"Send it all back, Winston."
"Are you certain, Madam?" Winston asks. "It was custom-made especially for you."
"It's the holiday season, darling. It simply isn't festive enough."

Living in the city at Christmastime is magical. But whenever we go out, we seem to attract a LOT of attention.

A spot finally opened up at the school Auntie Sprinkles wanted me to attend. My first day is tomorrow. I'm really excited and really nervous at the same time.

"Auntie Sprinkles, do you think the other kids will like me? I mean, I'm… different."

"Of course, they will, darling," Auntie Sprinkles says. "Remember, everyone is different in their own wonderful way. Just be your unique self, and trust me, they'll be fighting over you."

Things are going pretty well until our teacher, Mrs. Higgins, announces it's time to rehearse for the holiday play. To my surprise, the performance is only two days away!

I know I'm a unicorn, but not all unicorns like to be the center of attention. Secretly, I was hoping there weren't any roles left and Mrs. Higgins would let me sit this one out. Boy, was I wrong!

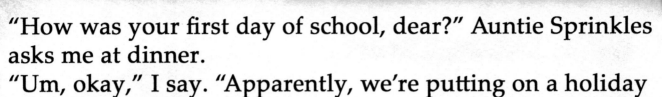

"How was your first day of school, dear?" Auntie Sprinkles asks me at dinner.

"Um, okay," I say. "Apparently, we're putting on a holiday play in two days."

"A holiday play? Oh, how marvelous!" Auntie Sprinkles says with an enthusiastic clap. "I assume you're the lead?"

"Well, no," I say, shrinking in my chair. "I'm… a tree."

"A tree?!" she exclaims.

"Yes," I say. "A Christmas tree. It was the only part left."

"Well, then," she says, standing up suddenly, "you'll be the most exquisite Christmas tree the stage has ever seen. Winston, please fetch my cape!"

Auntie Sprinkles has a surprising number of tips on how to be a Christmas tree.

The next day, we rehearse on the gym stage. When I put on my costume the other kids giggle. As Mrs. Higgins wraps lights around me, she explains that I'm the grand finale. First, she'll darken the stage, and then I'll go out and click the button to dazzle the audience with my holiday lights.

I want to do a good job, but when it's time to click the button the lights don't turn on.

"It'll be okay," Mrs. Higgins says reassuringly. "We'll have it fixed for the performance."

I nod, but I'm not so sure.

Later that night, I feel butterflies in my stomach.

"Auntie Sprinkles, what if the lights don't work tomorrow?"

"Oh, darling," she says, "please, don't worry."

"But won't everyone laugh at me?" I ask.

"Petunia, my little flower," she says, "they might laugh. But when things in life don't go your way, never, ever, let it dim your sparkle. If you embrace who you are, you will always know exactly what to do. And besides, you're a Fluffybottom!"

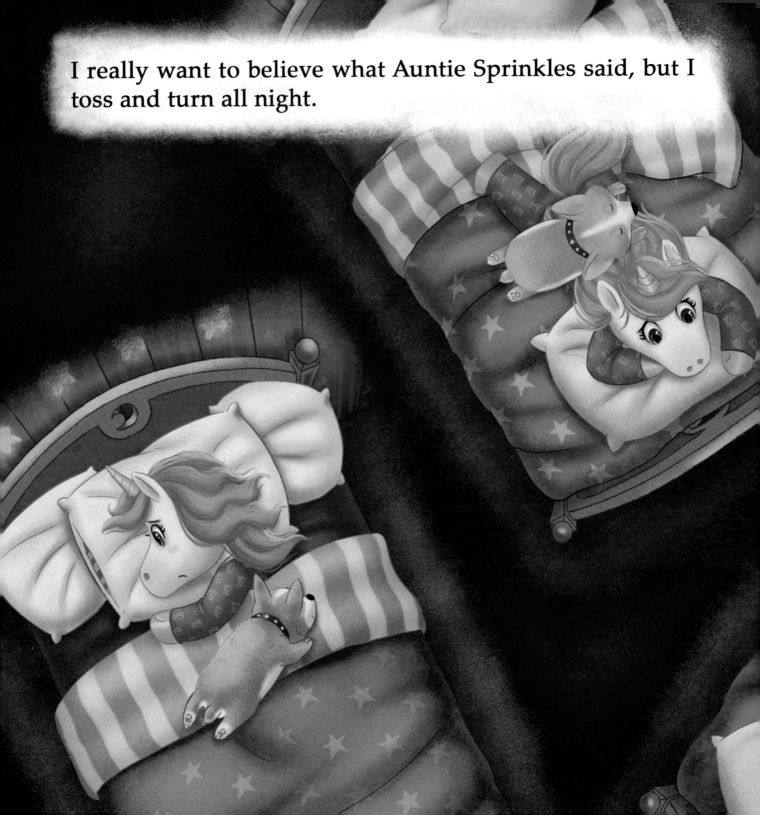

I really want to believe what Auntie Sprinkles said, but I toss and turn all night.

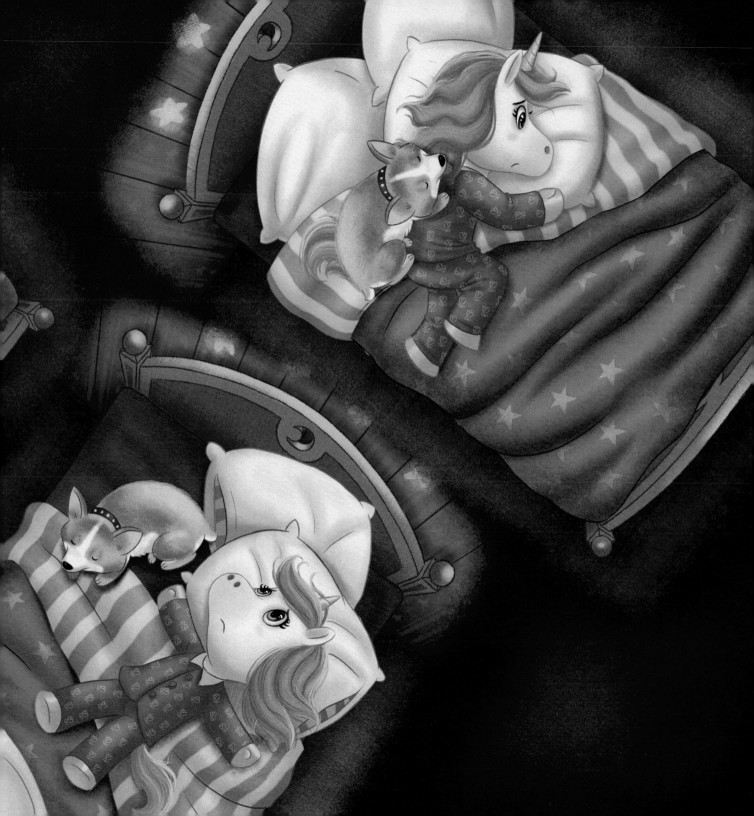

Before I know it, it's showtime! The gym is packed and my heart is beating fast. I wish I could just disappear.

Finally, it's time for the big ending. As Mrs. Higgins dims the lights, I take a deep breath and walk out on stage. Then, I click the button. And click it again. And again. AND AGAIN. Oh no! Where are the lights?

Everyone is staring at me and I start to panic. But then I see Auntie Sprinkles' smiling face and feel a sense of calm. Maybe she was right. Maybe I don't have to let this dim my sparkle. Besides, I'm a Fluffybottom! Wait, that's it! Suddenly, I know exactly what to do!

And that's when I realize that if I believe in myself, I can handle anything. After all, there's only one Petunia Cupcake Fluffybottom in this world, and I'm sure glad it's me!

R.L. Ullman is the bestselling author of award-winning books for kids. He creates fun, engaging characters that kids (and adults) want to read about. R.L. lives with his wife, son, two dogs, and a laptop in Connecticut. Find out what R.L. is up to at rlullman.com.

Yusup Mediyan is a freelance illustrator and animator who lives in West Java, Indonesia. He has illustrated children's books, book covers, and several animated series. He is also a father of two.

Reviews are important to bring this book to the attention of more readers. So, if you enjoyed this book, we would be very grateful if you could leave an honest review online. Thanks for your support!

Made in the USA
Middletown, DE
23 December 2022